FOREWORD

As George's project manager, I had the privilege of seeing firsthand how deeply he loved his wife in the way he spoke of her, in the way he chronicled every mile of their RV Journey. His records weren't just notes of travel; they were a testament to devotion. Every destination, every meal, every sunset was shared with her in his heart.

When I first opened his travel journals, I realized this wasn't a simple story about places - it was a story about partnership, gratitude, and the kind of love that outlives even time. This project honors both of them: the road they traveled, and the love that made every journey meaningful.

May this book remind us of all that love, once given truly, never ends. It just changes form and continues to travel on Everywhere Together.

DEDICATION

For George, every mile, every moment and every memory. I want to dedicate this traveling Journey to my wife whose continues to support, love and backing me in every situation that glued us together, no matter where we are.

EVERYWHERE TOGETHER

OUR JOURNEY OF

LOVE AND

Adventure

GEORGE REIDY

EVERYWHERE TOGETHER:

OUR JOURNEY OF LOVE AND ADVENTURE

By

George Reidy

PROLOGUE
Though her voice has quieted, her love still echoes in every mile.

George, this is our story-our journey of love and laughter, of roads traveled and moments cherished. I write these words with gratitude for the life we shared, for every sunrise that found us side by side, for every quiet night beneath the stars. You were my partner, my strength, and my joy. Though you have gone ahead on the road I cannot yet follow, I carry your memory in every mile I travel.

TABLE OF CONTENTS

CHAPTER 1:
THE BEGINNING OF THE ROAD
"Every dream we chased began with her smile and my hand in hers."

Looking back at where we started our life on the road, I still find myself feeling excited that there was a lot of pleasure in me and the day I had set my mind with my loving husband George to get rid of the normal lives that we lived back at home and enter into the world of the RV. We had not made a rush settlement as we planned, prayed, packed and re-packed! Nevertheless, despite all the careful consideration, the feeling of adventure was still there, as though we were venturing in a new chapter of life that has already been predetermined to us.

George always was the pragmatic one, the hand on the wheel, literally and figuratively. It was me who had been the dreamer, the one who had noticed beauty in the sunrise of a campground and poetry in an indefinitely long dusty road.

We were like a similar mindset and thrilled to experience something new in life with each other. We had lived through storms of life and yet our marriage had encountered every obstacle, which only seemed to increase the intensity of our mutual love and enhanced our trust in one another.

***

The first time we were discussing RV life, I believed that George was joking. I recall laughing and saying,

"You mean camping? At our age?"

But my husband had that same eye when he fooled me many years ago.

"It is not camping, sweetheart, It's freedom." George Said.

***

I could not forget that word, freedom. The more we trust each other, the more I think that George was right. We were not fleeing anything. We were being drawn to something new. We had something to do on the open road, and I did not know what I had been experiencing of. I was experiencing a silent calmness when we started to plan our RV adventurous life.

***

I do not know where to start. We did not begin our journey with some great statement or a carefully drawn map on the kitchen table. No, it was developing quietly, as the first light of day rose upon the horizon, promising everything would shine. We were not the sort to rush off after crazy aspirations with a wanton disposition; we relaxed into them, and held hands, and hoped that the next mile would show the way.

The idea actually took root in the winter of 2011. We had been talking about it for so long, had we not? Leaving the day-to-day routine behind, getting rid of all the things we didn't need and off to the open road in our RV that we lovingly called Adventure. You never uttered it, but with that light in your eye, as though the very mention of the name were an invitation to some adventure. You'd tease me when I told you adventure awaits, my love, and I would roll my eyes, passing off as the practical one. But deep down, I was thrilled. We had grown up, endured the tempest of life, and now, in our golden years, we felt that the universe was presenting us with a second delight in the wonder.

***

As Christmas came near that year, the suspense was piled on the windowsill. Me and George were not going out of house yet. We were already strained by our New York origins, but we were already testing our feet in the nomadic lifestyle by taking brief journey in the RV. We celebrated on a very small rolling house on the 24th of December 2011, where we were parked and there were twinkling lights in a canopy. I recall having grilled such rack of pork outdoors, the crackling combined with the aroma of California wine boiling the broccoli and corn.

You did the grilling so well George, with the tossing of the meat, which was of exaggerated style, and I made cherry chocolate rice Krispies as a dessert. Surely, you don't need a fancy dining room when I have this for you, my love George. He jested, pointing to my temporary installation in the RV.

So, we turned on the television to the Yule log and heard Christmas music as we lit candles and hung stockings in the front windows with a red one to you, a green one to me, and even a Santa hat swinging about. Our Amish Heat Surge heater (which we would later return, cursed be its inefficient heart) was fluttering in the background, with the little Christmas tree of Charlie Brown proudly standing on the table, ornaments of chocolate dog hanging on the tree, sent by PetSmart. Outdoors, even though the rain had been cold all day we had five white bags of sand and lights along the journey. We lighted up our own luminaria for the Festival of Lights celebration. Lights fluttered valiantly in the damp night as they shed a bright light that reflected the happiness in my heart.

That night, we were sitting together, fully satisfied and I had a feeling of gratitude. I said to you, "Merry Christmas, George, and leaned over your shoulders. You gripped my hand and your fingers as usual. We were going to have dinner at Chinese restaurant the following day, nothing fancy, only me and my loving husband George, enjoying the simple things. However, at that time I realized that this was the beginning of something greater. It was not a life escape trip. It concerned a wholeheartedness in its embrace.

***

By the beginning of 2012, the planning was in overdrive.

We would study maps at night, George, your fingers following roads all over Texas and further, and I wrote on notes campgrounds and places to visit. So, what about Rio Grande Valley? What would you recommend my love, rounding your eyes and smiling at the thought of nice people and cheap activities. I would nod, and into it I would add practical information such as fuel stops and care of our dear Rosy Sally, our pet dog who was as happy as we were or at least, she was tossing her tail eagerly at the thought of new smells.

***

We left home in late March. The van was full of necessities and some luxuries. We were anxious as we drove out of the driveway, saying goodbye to the old streets. "Adventure begins!" You know, George, you said, honking the horn like a kid on your first bike ride. I laughed and my heart was fluttering with nerves and joy. With faith in one another, trust in the highway, and faith in the Lord above, we headed off to south and to the world that was opening itself in front of us as we achieved our intended destinations.

***

The first actual experience of the road was on April 1, 2012, when we drove through Alamo, Texas. The hot air greets transition of the cold north. The kilometers were rocking around 47,530 when moving north on US 281 and palm trees were planted on either side of the road like guards. I replied,

9

and said, see that love, greener than the Valley, George replied, indicating the green country. But alas, the grumbling began early, did they? Water streaming on the spigot as she drove there, the size of Rosy Sally attracting side-eyes (and we put on one glance after another), the pool table farce with a little band of travelers invading our private game. We laughed at it later; you are playing the scowls with the lifeless frowns. The next time we took our band, I teased George.

***

The clubhouse was eccentric and had a leaky roof, with heavy rain, pool balls that did not fit perfectly, and sticks whose tips broke and were protruding on the wall. But we laughed at the mistakes. Eating table, such as Thanksgiving pork and ham (which, by the way, led me to diarrhea. But thanks for your sympathies and hugs, my loving husband). On Tuesday, we had jam sessions where we would knock our feet for free music. It was part and parcel of the adventure, and it taught us to take the punches.

On this particular night we were held at the border crossing three lanes deep, at 4:25 PM, cameras X-raying our truck, dogs sniffing fer contraband. "How many on board? The US citizens?" guard questioned, and at 4:41 we were on our way. It reached 99, then 100 degrees, the diesel cost $4.09 a gallon, and we drove on, over Alice, Texas, where the heat was rattling in my head like a mirage. You had seen a large herd of Brahman grazing in the open without shade or water, and I was plagued with sympathy. I grumbled, Oh Tough life out here, thank God we have our air-conditioned refuge.

We overtook a ruined tire from some other motor showroom, and as we passed George tossed out his black water hose on the road, but he shook his head. You said gruesome predicament, and we laughed at each other, promising to check our own tires more frequently. We believed in preparation, and we said our road motto.

We had spent the night of April 2 in a parking lot in Floresville, having supper at Bill Miller BBQ, where there was beef brisket that melted in our mouths. The cops patrolled round, and nobody knocked on the door. A mere evening with stars in the sky. The following day, a vet comes to see Rosy Sally: preventive heartworm, painkillers against her arthritis, Imodium should she have problems with her stomach. "Stop by in two years?" then suggested the assistant, and we grinned, and asked ourselves where the road would go at that time.

***

On the way to San Antonio, the landscape changed to overhead trains to carry coal cars and power plants to steam. I could never get over George, your attention to detail. You would indicate the turbines which produce electricity and I would be thinking about how we were moving in our own lives. We explored passageways with minimal difficulty, your gentle hand guiding the wheel as a path of silent confidence as we move and explore nature with me.

***

SAS shoe factory tour in San Antonio was an eye-opener on April 3, where the manufacturing process of shoes. We went back to the store carrying grips, and I got a version of black SAS tennis shoes (factory defect but made of steel). The clerk went as far as to include churros cookies! Then you grinned, "Texas hospitality," and I was grateful to these little favors that were sprinkled on the way.

Traffic slowed down during rush hour, but we laughed at it and we came in at the 12:30 tour at the right time. Conversations with other visitors such as grandpas telling us about their surgeries, clerks complaining of language barrier, also made our beautiful journey even more beautiful. "Push 1 for English!" George laughed at me, imitating phone voices and we burst into laughter.

***

We ate Schwan garlic shrimp and Mexican pineapple that evening as we parked at Cabela in the midst of noisy trucks. We had just been getting through a hailstorm by minutes, and the NBC news reported that the tornadoes were raging 200 miles towards north. Close call, I said, snugging up. George, you were my anchor, something that brought me back to reality that you and I could do anything together.

***

We joined the Fegans to lunch on April 5 and visited the house and museum of Henry. Roger Davis was a driver who took us on a tour of the truck and at every turn of the wind, he pulled a prank and even pushed a fire pole. On the following day, we ate BBQ at Bleeker's, which was an expensive, yet satisfying meal, and then paid them a visit to their new house. Rosy Sally had a sloppy journey, but Sally was cleaned with love, and we all blamed no one, but that is some of the magic of pet parenthood.

***

On Easter Sunday at the Fegans and ham dinner, wine, brownies saturated us with love. Their attic basement bedroom brought laughter, and we talked at least until 11.30, happy to have old friends in new locations.

We filled up propane and parked in the meat market at Granzin and got tender steaks and fajitas. I wondered back about the beginning of our adventure; we had set out home with a kind of excitement in our hearts and put our faith in one another. My loving husband humorously and patiently tolerated my diarrhea or pains in my shoulders. George, though, was my strength and my satisfaction. During the initial miles, we created memories that propelled us all the way.

***

Now with hindsight, I can see how it all started in those uncomplicated times togetherness over a cup of coffee, laugher around the twinkling of Christmas lights and that nudge of fate that gently whispered, *"Why not now?"*

CHAPTER 2
FINDING OUR RHYTHM

"She taught me that love's rhythm isn't in perfection — it's in patience."

George, why do I now smile while looking back on those early days down the road. We were like two kids who were learning to ride a bicycle and at first, we would be scraped and giggled as we lost our balance, but as we gained balance through the fun that had its own adventure. We made our RV as our rolling home, our small cocoon, on which we would ride through the storms and sunrise, naming it, with all the optimism in our hearts with our adventure.

It was not always smooth, there were some bumps, both literal and figurative, but all of them helped us to learn something valuable. We also learned to have faith in the journey, laugh at our blemishes, to embrace one another tenderly and with kind hearts towards each other. During such times, we grew in love, which was a part of the miles that we had to cover.

***

You cannot have adventures, you see them coming, you joke, and you tugged the speed-gauge. We slept that night at the Marriott in Armory Square, me doing the booking, you making jockey of the tow dolly. But what a small accident it

15

was when we saw the hotel car park was too small to experience the full Adventure!

***

We went around the parking two times, laughing that we did not gauge ahead. Live and learn, my love, I said, and holding your hand. We parked on a side street and as we strolled back hand in hand, I was thankful that you were there with me George.

We headed to new beginnings that night under the hotel lights, hoping that the road would burn what we required.

On the following day, August 14th, we left Marriott to go to Camping World where there was no fee, but free open areas and fun. However, learning to live in an RV requires learning the unhooking ritual. You took the broom and brushed out the hanging rubbish on the trees, and you were the sensible one, and I had called in advance to more promising places. Site unsuitable, you said in your scornful way, and both of us fell a-laughing, the leaves falling upon us like confetti.

***

On the 16th, after searching about, we arrived at Site 120 at Green Lake and paid $93 for one night. The silence there was soothing, George as you sat and watched the sunset over the water, telling me a few of the stories of our youth. I wondered at that time how we had come out of our city days. And this was our beat coming out, camp after camp. Even little incidents such as being forgetful and leaving the awning unchained taught us the lesson of patience, and your kind-hearted gestures always took off the burden from me. You would say, Adventure has spirit, patting the RV like an old friend.

***

On August 20th we were at Bass Lake, where there was no fee this time, which was like a gift from the universe. In the morning, we took our coffee in hand, planned how to spend the day and the afternoons, such as our trip to the Visitors Center at the Bathe I Bes Cemeton Hill on the 6th of September. But not without laughs and mischiefs. Gerorge, you recall we lost our way on the way to We Hustours, VA., as on September 3rd. GPS gave us the wrong direction, and we found ourselves in a blind street in an agricultural road. Why, that is, dear one, we have to be pioneers, you laughed, so that we turn us round with that unfading faith in our collaboration.

On the 4th we canceled an appointment with PA Cassady, in order to take the next adventure of the road. I was thankful to be picnicking by the roadside and sharing grilled chicken and stories. Such instances reminded me how life on the road deprived us of those things which were not necessary and gave us space to love and to enjoy and make memories that are shown as reflection in future.

***

September also came with rearrangements and minor accidents that currently ensure I smile in a gentle manner. On 11th we requested at Campground Greenville, VA, 186, 188, 190, or 191. Nut was left with something worse. The next time we will be pickier, I teased, you nodded. On the 12th we, after settling in at Fraud Resorts (what a name!), laughed at a slight fraud warning on our card. Next was the 13th, a night at ARRV Basle town under Passport America only at 18 dollars a night. But the true rhythm-finder was Long Branch Quiet Scenic Return Center between 14th and 17th and $34 in the old peaceful times. We walked, gently, your hands in my hand, thinking of how the highway resembled our marriage, the turns and twists of it, yet all along the same road.

A minor accident: leaving the water hose adapter behind causing a drippy connection. I can make the dream work, as you put it, said by me smiling in a syntactic fashion. I have put all my trust in you, George; in your ingenuity I had pegged my trust.

***

From the 14th to 19th of Mid-September, we reached Big Buck Resort in Hornsby, TN, Site 73 at a steal of $2.97 with Coast-to-Coast perks. However, the laughs came when we ordered a place the next time it would be the one when we were next to an icy place! There was mud on our shoes, and we followed it into the house, giggling like newlyweds. First mud

18

bath of adventure, I said. To adjust was to learn RV etiquette, such as cleaning up after Rosy Sally, who was our loyal friend. She contributed to her misfortunes, such as running after the squirrels and knocking on the picnic table almost. At ARR Little Rock AR Site #3, evening walks, eating together, spaghetti, chocolate cake had become a regular part of our routine after the price of the stay came to $36 at the 19th. One night I wrote in my journal about insomnia, but your constant breathing beside me was good enough for support and courage.

***

On the 1st of October, we arrived at Casa Del Valle and registered as newcomers by your phone under Reilly--they thought you were Rall! We laughed at nametags and Kelly and Donald tours. You would say, not telling how it was born in US with NY tags, mysterious. Site 705 was not suitable because there was rubble all over. After a brief conversation we went to 224. The disengagement of the tow dolly was a ball; you are sweeping and scouting on me.

Little accident-shaped personality, such as the incident I experienced with diarrhea, although we managed to deal with it and contemplated the vulnerability of life. By the 6th of October we had already settled, and we could see the difference, such as new chairs in the card room. Your power,

George, was there, that I had faith in your plans as we adapted to the life of the park.

***

Going back to 2012 momentarily, those recollections now mingle so well. In April we had plenty of things to laugh at. On the 1st, in Alamo, TX, we were in tacks over complaints about the dog pool and dirty showers. Poop always came, I defended Rosy, but did the pool table matter? When band came, we done a little prayer! I was left with a mishap such as diarrhea. But we meditated on plenty in the suffering. On our way to the north, border checks using X-ray cameras and snuff dogs were like a spy movie.

An overnight stay in a parking lot, with patrol by police with no interaction, since it was thankful to be safe. Vet checkup on Rosy: fuel refill costs $42.50 to have her hip dysplasia reminder to appreciate every wag. I was experiencing shoulder pain, and you were able to massage it away. By 3rd, there were 150 employees and 100 stages in SAS shoe factory tour in San Antonio. We had cookies and hangers. Traffic accident during rush hour: almost hit like a slugger.

***

At Cabela the 4th, the loud trucks all night, but we got adjusted with earplugs. Hailstorm flew by us with hope of luck. Diarrhea messes from Rosy? Accidents, though swept out with love.

20

May 2012 deepened our rhythm. Lyndon Baines Johnson Ranch on the 10th, easy 60s style, white Lincolns. Sauer Beckman farm: history alive, sheep and chicken to eat. Pacific War Museum on 11th with tiring yet magnificent site to visit. My birthday at your chicken supper in pistachio pie! It was our peaceful life lesson.

Guadalupe mountains 15th, complete, nauseous, but victorious hiking to 7,900 ft. Ranger's parking scold? Small mishap laughed off. Carlsbad Caverns on the 18th: Postcards and movie of the Big Room trail. Bats and white-nose syndrome are expressions of thankfulness to the wonders of nature.

***

On SKP RV "The Ranch" April 14th -25th happy hours with DVD nights. Windstorm dust accompanies accident but did not harm us. Remember George? You are concerned about my cramps too, love. My sales sweatpants and heating pad with Laundry, library movies find their place in the areas where we resided.

This is because as we wandered around, me and George, little accidents such as problems with payments or missteps were shared as laughingstock for both of us. Driving RV care, laughing at mud tracks, being thankful and thinking about it through our rhythm was love in motion. You were my compass and my joy. Always everywhere, everlastingly, my dear Husband George!

***

CHAPTER 3
CHRISTMAS ON WHEELS
"Her laughter still warms the coldest nights; she was home wherever we parked."

It was a cold wind blowing that evening in December, and the sort that winds about me and George and murmurs, "It's Christmas". The RV was a cozy and well-groomed parking place surrounded by flickering lights under a canopy at a small campground in Texas. It was our Christmas on the road, and it was our first holiday travelling together. And it was the coldest holiday we ever had.

Four wheels and a changing view with every sunrise had replaced the old, comfortable, but usual amenities of a standing house with my dear one, Me and my beloved husband. And still, even in that small motor home, with all the mismatched lights and the hiss of the heater, it seemed to be more of home than any brick-and-mortar house could have provided.

George had demanded to carry our little Charlie Brown Christmas tree. I liked its curvy little trunk and bare branches to laugh, particularly when he hung the Chocolate Dog Ornament in a ceremony, to celebrate with our great Rosy Sally dog. *"Every family needs a tree, he said, and every tree needs a dog".* I could not disagree with such reasoning.

***

Outside that night it was damp, the cold that creeped down to your bones. The entire day had been raining but the drizzle just served to make our small kingdom in the RV seem even more magical. The flickering light of tea candles was dancing back and forth, striking the aluminum siding, and creating dancing shadows on the ceiling. No less determined, George was at the grill in the rain outside, making the perfect Christmas dinner. I was at the window, and looking on him, working like a diligence man who is a royal banquet at the court, with George has Santa hat on one side.

As he entered inside, his eyes flushed and sparkling with red color, he bore the platter as a prize. "Ta-da!" George told me, laying it on our dining table which was also our little counter. Pork roast, steamed broccoli, corn, and stone-top dressing make the best dinner I ever had in my life. He fit as the King of the Road along with his Queen.

***

We laughed because we filled the glasses with California wine which did not match. We did not taste much, just love, eat to remain healthy, and to get where we go, although we did not know where that place would be.

Dinner was delicious, but the dessert made the night memorable. I remember watching George's eyes light up when he took the first bite. *"Now that's Christmas," he said, "with a snap, crackle, and pop."*

***

Outside, the luminarias glowed a string of white paper bags, each holding a cup of sand and a single tea candle, lighting up the walkway. We had set them out together earlier, shivering under umbrellas and laughing as the candles fought the wind. "They're our Farolitos," I said proudly, recalling the New Mexico tradition. *"A Festival of Lights, just for us."*

George nodded thoughtfully, his arm around me. "A home on wheels, but still home," he said.

Christmas morning greeted us with a soft drizzle and the sound of geese in the distance. We exchanged small gifts: I gifted George a leather keychain shaped like a camper, and he gave me a tiny silver locket with the engraving, "Every mile, together." Inside was a photo of us from our first stop at Bass Lake wind-blown, smiling, and completely unaware of how this adventure would shape us.

***

Instead of the traditional turkey dinner or family gathering, we went to a small restaurant in town. The owner, a cheerful man named Chen, wore a Santa hat over his apron and greeted every guest with a booming, "Merry Christmas!" We shared fried rice and hot tea, giggling over the fortune cookies that seemed to speak directly to us.

I read: *"Home is where the heart travels."* George said: *"A journey shared is twice travels with the joy."*

25

We stuck them on the dashboard later with tape, next to the map dotted with our travel stops. They became our motto for years to come.

Living in an RV had its quirks. Some days, the heater sputtered, or the awning refused to roll in, but we learned to laugh through it. Simple things became real treasures. Morning coffee brewed on a tiny stove, the hiss of the propane, Rosy Sally curled up on the passenger seat like a furry co-pilot.

We discovered that "home" wasn't a place as it was the way George would hum along to the radio while driving, or how I'd read aloud from a travel guide to keep us entertained on long stretches of highway. Home was wherever we parked, wherever laughter echoed between the cabinets and the curtains swayed to the rhythm of the road.

***

We found beauty in ordinary moments: washing dishes together in a metal sink no bigger than a shoebox, folding laundry at campground laundromats where strangers became friends, and taking walks at sunset under skies that looked painted just for us.

***

In Greenville, Virginia, a kind couple shared hot cocoa with us by their campfire. In Arkansas, a little boy gave Rosy Sally a red ribbon for her collar. At every stop, the world seemed to open its arms wider, welcoming us as wanderers with stories that held in my mind till today.

That first winter taught us more about love than any season before or after. We learned patience with the kind that comes when the generator did not function in the middle of the night and we just hold each other under blankets, whispering, "We'll figure it out tomorrow." We learned resourcefulness like how to fix a leaking faucet with duct tape, and my faith grew stronger in George's work. And most of all, we learned trust on each other with every mile towards our glamorous journey.

There were no walls between us, literally or figuratively. The RV was small enough that every breath, every sigh, every chuckle filled the space completely. When I laughed too hard, the lights flickered. It was imperfect, yet perfectly ours.

Sometimes, when the weather cleared, we'd set out folding chairs by the roadside and just watch the sunset. George would pour a bit of wine, and we'd toast to the horizon.

"We could be anywhere," he'd say, *"but as long as we're together, it's home."*

Even our Christmas lights stayed up long after the season passed. George called them our "traveling constellations." At every stop, he'd string them across the windshield, and each time they blinked, it felt like the universe was winking back at us.

***

Traveling together wasn't without its mishaps, and laughter was our best travel companion.

There was night in Casa Del Valle when George tried to go back to the RV a narrow campsite. *"A little to the left!"* I shouted. He went right. "No, the other left!" I corrected, waving my arms wildly. The RV stopped with a gentle bump against a low bush. George leaned out the window, grinning sheepishly. *"Looks like we're adventuring the landscapes tonight."*

We laughed until our sides hurt, then set up camp right where we landed. The next morning, our neighbors complimented us on the "creative parking job."

Then there was the time the hot water heater quit during mid-shower. I came out wrapped in a towel, hair dripping, muttering about "frozen shampoo." George just handed me a mug of coffee and said, "At least the coffee's hot." That became our phrase for any travel inconvenience: *"The coffee's hot."*

It was our way of saying, life may not be perfect, but there's always something good right in front of us.

***

That Christmas marked the beginning of many shared journeys across states, through seasons, and into years of adventure. But it was also a quiet revelation that love doesn't need grandeur or certainty to thrive. It grows best in motion, nourished by small joys and gentle laughter.

Looking back, I see that the beauty of that first holiday together wasn't in the gifts or the decorations. It was in the way we learned to slow down, to notice and to be grateful to God. Each day offered a new reason to give thanks and sometimes as simple as a sunrise, or the warmth of George's hand reaching for mine as the road stretched endlessly ahead.

Even now, when I hear the soft hum of tires on pavement or smell pine mixed with diesel, it brings me back to that Christmas on wheels and the laughter echoing in the cold night air, the flicker of candlelight through the foggy RV window, and the feeling that we were exactly where we were meant to be.

Years later, when I think about that winter, it's not the miles that stand out. It's the moments. The way George's eyes crinkled when he smiled. The way Rosy Sally wagged her tail at every new place, as if declaring, "This too is home." The way even the simplest meal felt like a feast when shared at our tiny table.

We were rich, not in possessions, but in peace. The kind of peace that comes from knowing that joy doesn't depend on circumstances. It flows from love, trust, and the grace of sharing life's journey together.

Our first holiday on the road became the compass for everything that followed. It taught us that laughter is the best travel gear, gratitude the most reliable map, and love the only true destination.

***

Even now, when I decorate for Christmas, I hang that little Chocolate Dog Ornament and whisper, "Here's to us, George to the road that never ends, and to love that still travels."

And, I imagine, loving George also smiles steadily at the wheel, Christmas lights twinkling in the windshield, and the road stretching on forever beneath us.

CHAPTER 4
THE WIDE-OPEN SKY

"Beneath every sky, I still feel her beside me —
free and forever."

On October 21, 2012, under the Endless Blue sky, me, and George, my love as I sit here piecing together our memories for this chapter, I can almost feel the gentle sway of Adventure, our faithful RV, rolling down those sunbaked highways. This part of our story, "The Wide-Open Sky," captures that magical stretch of our journey through the American Southwest in 2012. It was a time when the world opened up before us like a vast canvas, painted with deserts, mesas, and mountains that stretched to infinity.

We weren't just traveling; we were embracing freedom, the kind that comes from having no deadlines, no obligations beyond each other's company. The landscapes whispered peace to our souls, and in those shared moments of wonder, I felt our love deepen, like roots finding water in arid soil. Oh, how we laughed at the little mishaps, trusted the road ahead, and gave thanks for every breathtaking vista. Let's re-live those moments, mile by mile.

***

On April 14, 2012, we advance towards the Desert's Embrace at Lakewood, NM. Our adventure into the wide-open began as we pulled into "The Ranch" in Lakewood, New Mexico, after a dusty drive through scrubland that seemed to go on forever. The sky was a flawless dome of blue, so it made me feel small yet utterly free from stress and tensions. George, with his ever-present grin, parked Adventure in spot #9 on Lege Vista and unhitched the tow dolly, and said, "This is it, darling as our slice of nowhere!" I chuckled at his enthusiasm because George always had a way of turning ordinary words into poetry.

That first evening, we joined the happy hour at the clubhouse, sipping iced tea under a sunset that painted the distant hills in pinks and golds. The cool breeze was blowing, carrying the faint scent of sage. Rosy Sally, our furry companion, sniffed around the fenced sewage pool, even though it had a quirky charm. We met Donna, the welcoming clerk who gave me a golf cart tour, pointing out the laundry facilities and the vast emptiness beyond. "Nothing but sky and stars out here," she said. George and I exchanged a knowing look; that's exactly why we came here.

As night fell, we stepped outside for Adventure, hand in hand, gazing at the Milky Way sprawling above like a river of diamonds. "Remember when we thought city lights were the height of romance?" I teased him. George pulled me close, his laugh rumbling softly. "This beats any skyline, love. Here, we're just free as birds." In that peace, I felt a profound gratitude for our life on the road, trusting that whatever came next, we'd face it together.

***

On April 18, 2012, me and George landed at Artesia and its stunning view of Plains.

Feeling refreshed after a few days of rest as my shoulder ache eased and Rosy Sally's tummy troubles subsided when we reached Artesia. The drive was a symphony of open space: flat plains dotted with prickly pear cactus, low bushes, and the occasional rangy cow munching on what little green grass under our feet. The sky dominated everything, a boundless expanse that made the horizon feel like a filming scene.

In Artesia, we snapped photos of cowboy statues and bronze horses, laughing as George struck a dramatic pose beside one. "Yee-haw, partner!" he drawled in his best Western accent, which was hilariously something I couldn't experience before.

We wandered into Gregg's Food for groceries, splurging on antique pencil sharpeners and boots with small treasures to remind us of the day's whimsy. The heat climbed to 91 degrees, making me a tad nauseous, but George's steady hand on mine grounded me. "We've got all the time in the world," he said gently.

Back at The Ranch, we watched a Will Smith movie in Adventure's cozy interior, the deserted wind humming outside.

Reflecting on the day, I whispered my thanks for these simple joys, the freedom to explore without rush, the peace of vast landscapes that quieted my mind, and the wonder of sharing it with you, George. Your trust in the journey always inspired me.

***

On April 19, 2012, our plan was to adventure the Carlsbad Caverns that descent into Wonder.

Eighty miles north to Carlsbad Caverns, another day under that wide-open sky, now shimmering with heat waves. The landscape shifted from scrubby flats to rugged hills, mountains looming on the horizon like ancient guardians. We parked Adventure and descended into the Big Room and King's Palace, our footsteps echoing in the cool, subterranean world.

But oh, the surface! Emerging, we marveled at the contrast with the cave's mysteries below and the endless sky above. George held my hand as we walked the trails, Rosy Sally trotting ahead. "Imagine, all this formed over millennia," he mused, his voice full of awe. I nodded, feeling a shared wonder that bound us tighter. We bought postcards and watched a film on the caverns' origins, then drove back through scabby terrain, speed limit was 70 mph and wind whipped past through us.

That evening, as stars blanketed the sky, I reflected on the peace of such places. No crowds, no noise. It's just us, the land, and the freedom to breathe it in. "You're my greatest adventure," I told George, earning a tender kiss. Gratitude overflowed; how lucky we were to explore nature with plenty of misadventures that resulted in our laughs and moments of joy.

***

On May 14, George planned to see the beauty of Albuquerque and its mountains that folded into our memories like precious thing.

Shifting gears, we headed from Abiquiú toward Albuquerque, the Candia Mountains layering the horizon like stacked pancakes under a sky so blue it hurt the eyes. The seven-mile ride to Sandia Peak felt like ascending into heaven with freedom in every curve of the road. We stopped at the Santa Fe Travel Center, benches overlooking vista after vista, the Rail Runner train zipping by like a silver streak.

The trail leveled into wide paths through mountain passes, earth grooved by wind and time. "Look at that big view," George said, pulling over so we could soak it in. Peace settled over us like a warm blanket; no words needed, just shared silence. In Albuquerque, we dined simply, reflecting on the day's wonders, the vastness that made our worries small, the trust we had in each other's company. Humor crept in when George joked about the "abnormal" water prices in Italy from a random thought as our minds wandered freely here.

***

May 18, 2012, we decided to adventure the Mesa Verde and its Cliffs and Eclipses.

On to Mesa Verde National Park in Colorado, the sky a twilight canvas as we approached Cortez. Knife-edge ridges and thin rock formations defied gravity, the park's wonders unfolding under an immense dome. We toured Cliff Palace, George's energy boundless as he hiked the loops, while I savored the views from safer spots.

That annular eclipse day was magic with the moon covering the sun at 72% maximum, casting an ethereal light. Coyotes howled nearby, Sully (wait, Rosy Sally's playful alias that day) perked on her ears. "Nature's show just for us," George whispered, his arm around me. The peace was profound, and the shared wonder was electrifying. As shadows danced on the Mesa Verde, I felt gratitude for this freedom to witness such spectacles together and trust the universe's rhythm.

We dropped 2,000 feet, photographing stone gravity and rugged rises. At Witt RV Park, near a casino, we hooked up for $22, the glow of night lights a gentle end. Reflection came easy in these wide-open spaces, as our love felt as eternal as the sky.

***

On May 20th, we went to tour the Four Corners where world meets with a massive sky ahead of us.

The Four Corners monument was a tiny marker under the

vast sky, where Utah, Colorado, Arizona, and New Mexico converge. Flags flapped in the breeze, tourists posing in shade, but for us, it was a symbol of boundless freedom. The landscape was immensely beautiful. The brown rock layers tilting and sandbars sagging in heat, yet mesmerizing in its infinity.

George and I stood, each foot in a different state, laughing hysterically. "We're everywhere at once!" he quipped. The nothingness of the canyons stretched endlessly, wind in our hair, and peace in our hearts. We drove on bumpy roads that felt like gliding on ice, zigzagging through pale formations and dusty greens. In Blanding, Utah, we considered a motel but opted for Adventure's comfort.

That night, under a star-studded sky, I reflected on the day's lessons with the beauty of America's landscapes and the wonder we shared in its vastness. Gratitude for George, my anchor in this freedom, who intensified me through gorgeous and breath-taking scenes. Trusting the road had brought us here and humor kept it light upon us.

The further adventure began in August of 2015, when we gathered in our known locations in New York, and headed out to the open country of the Midwest and the rest of the world. Our first visit to a doctor was on the 13th of August when we met with Dr. Downing at 12:45 PM, before we had checked in to the La Bass Lake Arv Hotel. You remember, George? We arrived with Tim Taylor of Auto Glass tinkering over the windshield and assuring that our vision before heading to the planned destination was vibrant and clear with everything available that matters as being a tourer.

***

On September 10, George struck with plan as usual, and we proceeded towards Hyatt's Green Acres with its stunning Plains.

It was back in the Midwest briefly, but the wide-open sky up and plains view under our feet, one could not except better site than this. At Hyatt's Green Acres in Albany, it was surrounded by cornfields and a small lake, the sky felt closer, like a loving embrace. Gopher holes dotted the clay-silt ground and George joked about "whacking" them like the owner, our laughter echoing across the fields.

We shared campfire stories with an older couple, the husband a quiet veteran with war tales. A raccoon clawed at Adventure's ceiling one night with hilarious chaos! "Our uninvited guest," George chuckled, shooing it away. The peace of those starry nights and the freedom of rural simplicity filled us with wonders. I trusted our journey's twists and grateful for every shared sunrise and sunset we saw together.

***

On September 20th, we parked our RV at Cabela with the permits of Weapon.

At Cabela's lot in a rainstorm, George browsed goods while I marveled at the sky clearing to reveal endless blue.

"Handguns and horizons," he teased, navigating residency proofs for a permit. Humor in the absurdity with mobile life under wide skies.

We drove through cornfields, challenging winds but landscapes were stunning. Fuel at $3.99, and no cost for all the joys and adventures we done. We found peace in the vastness, wonder in nature's scale and gratitude for George's steady presence in my life.

***

On October 2, our trip towards Mississippi Valley set the adventure on our heads.

Overlooking the Mississippi near Dubuque, Iowa, the sky mirrored with the river's expanse. Fields of wildflowers, maple trees rolling like European countryside with beauty that stirred the soul. At Field of Dreams, smaller than the movie but magical under open skies hold my sight for many hours after wondering about the immaculate scenery.

We boondocked at Mystique Casino, with cold winds howling, but wrapped in blankets, we laughed through it. Freedom in spontaneity, peace in shared warmth, wonder at America's landscapes. Reflecting on our path, it was done with trust and love that guided and held us together.

George, these dates blur into one glorious tapestry under

the wide-open sky. Your gentle spirit, humorous quips, and unwavering trust made every landscape a love letter. I'm grateful for the peace we found, the wonders we shared. Forever together, in freedom's embrace.

***

CHAPTER 5
THE PEOPLE WE MET
"She saw kindness in everyone, and through her eyes, so did I."

Oh, George, if our RV "Adventure" was the vessel that carried us across this vast country, it was the people we encountered along the way who truly steered our hearts. In campgrounds and quiet roadside stops, we found not just fellow travelers, but kindred spirits with strangers who became friends in the span of a shared sunset or a potluck dinner. They reminded us that kindness is the quiet glue holding humanity together, often appearing when we least expected it, but most needed it. With gentle humor and unwavering trust, we opened ourselves to these connections, and in return, we were gifted with stories, laughter, and lessons that enriched our journey.

Our travels in 2011 were like a gentle prelude, George, where the road taught us to trust in the serendipity of human encounters. Remember that chilly December evening on the 24th of December, when we grilled rack of pork in our RV, the aroma mingling with Christmas carols from the TV.

We stepped outside to light our luminarias with those simple white bags with tea candles glowing softly in the wet cold. It was then that Sheri Lall, our campground neighbor from Muskogee, Oklahoma, wandered over with her Lebanese dog, Rosie (whom she affectionately called her "Doogie"). She recited a playful poem she'd written: "There is a Sally, so Rosy / Four legs, a tail and quite nosey / From Muskogee, this Okie, / Great Lebanese Doogie on my heart so I gave her a Hogie!" We laughed a lot with the kind of gentle humor that warms you from inside brings out the stress or any mental fatigue.

Sheri shared stories of her own solo travels, her gratitude for simple joys like a shared fire, and in that moment, we felt the trust of instant camaraderie. She even joined us for cherry chocolate rice krispies dessert, reminding us that strangers could become family under the holiday lights. Your eyes twinkled as you said, "See? The road gifts us these gems." How grateful I am for that night as it set the tone for the connections to come.

***

By 2012, our journey had picked up pace, and so did the people who colored it. In April, as we navigated Texas highways, we pulled into L51 Ron Runes Campground near Alamo on the 1st. The complaints started small like leaky spigots, unclean showers, but it was human kindness that turned it around. Stirlay, an older gentleman with a weathered face and a twinkle in his eye, overheard us grumbling about the pool table's mismatched balls and broken cues. "Life is like that table," he chuckled gently, "dimples and dips, but you play anyway." He spent the afternoon fixing what he could, sharing stories of his days in the military, and even invited us to a shared meal of Thanksgiving leftovers (though I got a touch of diarrhea. Our shared laugh over that mishap bonded us).

George's quiet trust in helping strangers restored my faith in the road's generosity. We left with hugs and old gentleman's number, grateful for how he turned frustration into friendship.

Later that month, on the 2nd, we overnighted at Bill Miller BBQ in Floresville, parking in a less-lit-down lot. The police patrolled, but instead of shooing us away, an officer named Dr. Brumluwi (yes, with his wife Nancy, who was as skinny as a rail but full of fire) stopped to chat. He checked on our dog Rosy Sally, prescribing butazol for her arthritis with a humorous warning: "Don't let her chase too many squirrels or she'll outrun you both!" Their kindness extended to a vet visit where Nancy shared her own pet stories, fostering a connection born of shared love for animals. We trusted their advice, and Rosy's hips improved. Their sincere gratitude for gentle guidance lingers always in my heart.

***

Mid-April brought us to Cabela's in Buda, where we met Babu Dave and Barb Fegan on the 3rd. Oh, George, the humor in that noisy truck-filled lot! Dave, with his booming laugh, joined you for a trip to Granzin's meat market, returning with steaks and fajita strips that we grilled together. Barb hosted an Easter dinner on the 8th, complete with ham, wine, and brownies, introducing us to their family-Dan, Carrie, Chris,

Shay, David, and Mathew. Amid the chaos of kids and stories, Barb's reflection on life: "We're all just passing through, but connections make the stay worthwhile" that struck deep in all of us. We stayed up till 11:30, sharing laughs over Rosy Sally's diarrhea mishaps (poor girl, but it became our inside joke). Their trust in opening their home to us wanderers filled us with gratitude as it was human connection at its next level.

***

As May dawned, we ventured to Lyndon Baines Johnson Ranch on the 10th, where a spiritual ranger (whose name escapes me now) shared tales of LBJ's Lincolns and family legacy with such gentle passion. His admiration was infectious, and we lingered, reflecting on leadership and kindness. Later, at the Sauer-Beckman farm, we met Christine Sauer's descendants, who spoke of their 10 children and midwifery days. Their stories of resilience connected us to history's human thread.

By mid-May, at SKP RV "The Ranch" in Lakewood from the 14th to 25th, Dunna the clerk gave us a golf cart tour, her humor shining as she pointed out the "sewage pool" with a wink: "Fancy, huh? But the views make up for it." Happy hours at 4:15 PM brought free iced tea and conversations with fellow RVers stories of dust storms and War Horse DVDs shared under starry skies. One Tuesday, I battled cramps, and a kind stranger brought me a heating pad, their quiet act of compassion, a reminder of trust in campground people whom we met across our entire journey. Gratitude washed over me as we sang and shared, George-you always joined in with your off-key enthusiasm.

***

June and July saw us at Guadalupe National Park, where Ranger Pate gently scolded us for parking woes on a busy weekend but helped rearrange spots with a smile. His kindness turned potential tension into laughter. At Carlsbad Caverns on the 18th, we met tour guides who whispered about white-nose syndrome in bats, fostering reflections on nature's fragility and human stewardship.

***

September brought deeper bonds. At Hyatt's Green Acres in Albany from August 14th to September 10th, the owners shared campfires with us and an older couple-the husband, a quiet giant missing a leg, swapped war stories with you, George. His "whooshing" apologies over lost matches had us in stitches, a gentle humor amid gratitude for shared vulnerability. A raccoon incident led to laughs and rent negotiations, strengthening our trust in these fleeting friends.

In Mitchell, South Dakota, from the 11th, Dumise and her family including Nick, Ottinel and Kristi welcomed us to their church, sharing sermons and survival kits. Amy's graceful conversations on faith and hope, and Naomi's youthful energy, connected us spiritually. Their kindness including us wanderers filled with reflection of life's mirrors that how people reflect our best selves.

***

By 2015, our journey felt more poignant, George, as health whispers reminded us of time's fragility. In October, at Casa Del Valle from the 1st, Kelly and Donalds treated us like newcomers (thanks to your phone mix-up as "Reilly"-oh, the humor in your "Rall" nametag!). Joseph the manager hurried away, but their tour and warm welcome fostered instant trust. Neighbors like Bill (with his yellow golf cart and card games) and Dan (removing our dolly after complaints) showed kindness in small acts, connecting us through shared campground quirks. My appreciation for their gentle acceptance runs deep because it was as if they knew we needed that warmth.

***

As our travels looped through New Mexico and beyond meeting Antonio Garcia advocating for water conservation, Maria Garcia Gonzalez the eager park ranger at San Felipe trails, and Ruby's determined stride on rocky paths-these encounters wove a tapestry of human kindness. In 2012's Mesa Verde, Sully the dog's coyote standoff with us sparked reflections on awareness and presence. By December 2012 in St. Augustine, Park Ranger Gunner Sargent's cannon

46

reenactment connected us to history, while Peter Gold's junk art and the Love Tree symbolized intertwined lives. Craig's Indigenous insights on the 11th invited gentle reflection on identity.

And then, George, the heartbreak of Rosy Sally's passing on December 13th, 2012, at Trout Creek RV Park. Vickie, Debbie, and Randy's compassion for helping with arrangements amid their own changes has embodied trust and connection in grief. Their quiet support reminded me that even in loss, people hold us up.

Looking back, these souls-campground friends, strangers turned confidents, taught us gratitude for the road's gifts. You, George, with your loving trust, opened doors to these bonds. In reflection, I see how human kindness illuminated our path, a gentle humor in mishaps, profound gratitude in shared moments. We're everywhere together, forever connected through them.

As I reflect on these moments now, my appreciativeness overflows; George you always said, "People are the real adventure," and how right you were.

***

CHAPTER 6
LESSONS FROM THE JOURNEY
"Together we learned that every detour has its purpose, and every mile its mercy."

Our RV "Adventure" could talk about what stories it would tell! Not just of the miles we traveled or the sunsets we chased, but of the bumps in the road with literal and figurative that tested us, bound us closer, and taught us the art of rolling with life's unpredictable turns. This chapter is my love letter to those moments that show how we both travel, adventure and remain patient in every difficulty that comes our way, my never-ending love George. The ones where we faced challenges head-on, leaned on each other like two old oaks in a storm, and emerged wiser, laughing at our own follies. Through it all, I learned that patience isn't just waiting-it's trusting the journey, and resilience is the quiet strength we built together. Let's revisit those roads, year by year, and reflect on the lessons they whispered to our hearts.

The Spark of Teamwork in Holiday Chaos started innocently enough on December 24, 2011, our first Christmas in "Adventure." You grilled that rack of pork to perfection, George, while I fussed over the cherry chocolate rice krispies dessert. The RV was aglow with lights, our little Charlie Brown tree twinkling, and outside, we lit those luminarias and the cold rain. But oh, the challenges! The Amish Heat Surge heater we bought turned out to be a dud and destined for return and the rain turned our setup into a soggy mess. I remember you chuckling as we dashed inside, dripping wet, only to find the TV blaring Christmas carols a bit too loud. "Well, at least the pork didn't drown," you said with that signature grin.

That night taught us our first big lesson in teamwork: dividing tasks without stepping on each other's toes. You handled the grill like a pro, while I orchestrated the indoor festivities. When the heater failed, we didn't panic; we huddled under blankets, toasting to our "cozy" mishap. Patience came in waves and waiting for the rain to pour on us, trusting that our imperfect setup was still perfect because we were in it together. As I see now, George, it built our resilience. We learned to laugh at the little disasters, turning them into cherished memories. Gratitude filled my heart on that holiday. For you, my steady partner, and for the simple joy of building our traditions on wheels.

***

By April 1, 2012, we were deep in Texas, navigating the Rio Grande Valley's endless highways. Remember that border inspection backup, George? We sat there, engine humming, as the sun baked us. Diesel was $4.09 a gallon-ouch! and the heat climbed to 100 degrees. Then, just outside Alice, TX, we spotted that gruesome scene: a motorhome with a shredded tire, black water hose strewn across the road. "Could be us," I whispered, but you squeezed my hand. "Not with our teamwork, love."

That day epitomized road challenges with unpredictable delays, mechanical woes lurking around every stop we headed for adventure. But we tackled them together. You checked the tires religiously after that, while I mapped alternate routes. Patience was key as we breathed through the waits, chatting about our dreams instead of fretting. Resilience shone when we hit Floresville that evening, parked in a dimly lit lot patrolled by police. No hookups, but we made do, sharing a quiet BBQ dinner from Bill Miller's. I was grateful for your calm presence, George. It turned potential stress into an adventure.

***

Fast forward to April 5, 2012, in Buda, TX, at Cabela's lot. Trucks rumbled all night, but we snuggled in, laughing about the "free concert." The next day, visiting the Fegans, our friends' new home sparked reflections on our nomadic life. Rosy Sally had diarrhea, the poor pup! -messing the hall, but we cleaned it up as a team, you rinse while I soaped. "Teamwork makes the dream work," you quipped, even as we yawned from lack of sleep. That week, with Easter at the Fegans' and Rosy's ongoing issues, tested our patience. We adjusted plans, opting for Hwy 71 RV Park when spots filled up. Learning together meant adapting: rice and bacon bits for Rosy and quiet evenings for us. Your resilience inspired me, George-vomiting after hiking Guadalupe Peak at 7,900 feet yet pushing on with a smile. "Would I do it again? Maybe," you said, knees sore but spirit unbroken. Trust grew as I knew we'd conquer any peak hand in hand.

***

May 2012 brought Carlsbad Caverns, NM-a magical descent into the Big Room. But the drive there? Desert scrub, low fuel, and Ranger Pate scolding us for "taking too much space" in the lot. We paid the fee, walked Rosy, and moved on, chuckling at the absurdity. Teamwork: you dump the tow dolly while I toured the visitor center. Patience in the heat, resilience in the isolation. At "The Ranch" SKP RV Park in Lakewood, a dust storm hit like a mini–Dust Bowl, coating everything in sand. I battled with cramps! But you shopped sweatpants and a heating pad, turning out to be a caretaker for me with gentle humor. "My Florence Nightingale," you teased me, George. Gratitude overflowed for your unwavering support, teaching me that true learning happens in vulnerable situations.

***

September 2012 in Iowa was a whirlwind of fairs and fields. At Freeborn County Fairgrounds on the 9th, we camped amid gopher holes with hilarious hazards! A raccoon clawed our ceiling one night, but we patched it with fun and laughter.

Then, Mitchell, SD, with its Corn Palace and Chinese buffets.

Rosy Sally's antics-smacking the kitchen key while we ate had us in stitches. But challenges arose when my knee injury, bleeding and pain and limiting me from walking. You took over dog duties, patient as ever. We visited Palmer Chiropractic College in Davenport on October 2, navigating admissions with Carrie Francis's help. Rainy drives on I-80, gift card glitches at breakfast and frustrations piled up. Yet, we learned resilience: cash backups, deep breaths. "We've got this," you'd say, trusting our bond.

***

By December 2012 in St. Augustine, FL, tragedy struck with Rosy Sally's passing. Her labored breathing, unresponsive limbs broke us. Racing to vets, pleading for help, but it was too late. We held her, reflecting on her lessons in patience (endless vet waits) and resilience (her fighting spirit). Teamwork in grief: you lift me while driving through tears. Gratitude for her life, and for you, George, my rock in the storm.

***

Fast-forward to August 2015, back in New York State at Green Lakes State Park. Site 120, $93 for the stay worth every penny for the serenity. But challenges with low-interest rate calls from CSG Solutions harassing us, and MyChart logins failing. We teamed up and you handling calls with firm politeness, me resetting passwords. Patience in the glitches,

52

resilience in persistence. Camping World visits, Bass Lake drives scenery soothed, but your assumed name "Rall" at Casa Del Valle sparked gentle humor. "From the US," you'd say mysteriously, tags from NY confusing folks. We laughed, learning to embrace our quirks.

***

September 2015 in Virginia: Gettysburg ARRV, free on Coast to Coast. Quiet sites, but shoulder pain plagued me. You uncoupled the tow dolly at site 705, deeming it unsuitable, then swept debris like a knight. Teamwork: me calling for alternatives, you scout. Patience in search, resilience in adapting to different places. Little Rock, AR, diesel at $2.29-bargain! But insomnia hit hard. Awake after 36 hours, I journaled gratitude for you and health with home on wheels. "I'll sleep eventually," I wrote, trusting the night would pass. You held me, whispering encouragement and teaching me resilience through care and affection.

***

In October 2015 at Casa Del Valle: they treated us as newcomers; we toured facilities with Kelly and Donald. Changes abounded new chairs, flooring but your "Reilly" registration mix-up had us giggling. "Assumed name tag: Rall," I teased. Road challenges: debris from trees and unsuitable sites. But we overcame, choosing site 224 together. Patience in the process, learning that flexibility that strengthens bonds between us. Gratitude for each shared mile, George.

Darling George, weaving these memories, I see how road challenges forged our teamwork like puzzle pieces clicking into place. From tire shreds in Texas to vet runs in Florida, we divided burdens, laughed at mishaps, and trusted each other's strengths. Patience wasn't passive; it was active waiting, breathing through storms and knowing dawn follows. Resilience that I have learned was all from you. Vomiting on peaks yet descending stronger; me, journaling through pain and emerging grateful. We learned together the adaptability in detours, humor in chaos and love in every mile.

***

Our "Adventure" wasn't just an RV. It was us, rolling resiliently and our hearts intertwined with every mile we took. I'm forever grateful, my ever-loving Husband, George. Wherever the road leads now, your lessons and presence always guided me in right direction.

***

CHAPTER 7
OUR FAITHFUL COMPANION
"Even our dog knew she was love itself — gentle, steady, and true."

Our sweet, loyal Rosy Sally. How do I even begin to capture the essence of you in these pages? You weren't just a dog; you were the heartbeat of our adventures: the furry glue that held George and me together through every twisty road and unexpected detour. From the moment we brought you home, with your wagging tail and those soulful eyes that seemed to say, "I'm with you forever," and you became our faithful companion. Your loyalty was unwavering, your antics were a source of endless laughter, and your quiet presence brings wellspring of emotional support during the quieter, more reflective moments of our RV life.

As I sift through our journals, rewriting these memories in the gentle glow of gratitude, I see how you taught us about trust, joy, and the simple beauty of life. George and I often joked that "Adventure," our trusty RV, had four wheels and one tail. It means about you, Sally. The journey back through the years, date by date, and relive those precious times with you by our side.

On December 24, 2011, our first holiday season on the road was magical, but it was you, Sally, who made it feel like home. That Christmas Eve, George and I nestled into "Adventure" with the TV playing soft carols and a Yule log flickering on the screen. But the real star was our little Charlie Brown Christmas tree, adorned with a chocolate dog ornament that looked just like you with perky leaves and mischievous grin. You sat there, tilting your head as if approving our humble setup and your tail thumping rhythmically against the floor.

George laughed as you nosed at the stockings we'd hung in the window with two red ones and a green, plus a Santa hat for good measure. "Sally thinks she's getting extra treats this year," George teased, scratching behind Sally's ears. And she did, of course. Your loyalty shone through in those quiet moments; while George and I shared stories of past Christmases, you curled up between us, your warm body, a reminder that family isn't just about people; it's about the bonds that fight with every storm.

That night, as we stepped outside to light luminarias in white bags filled with sand, you trotted alongside, sniffing the cold, wet air after a day of rain. It was freezing, but your enthusiasm warmed us. Merry Christmas indeed, with you as our faithful guardian against the cold and chilly weather.

We planned a Chinese restaurant outing the next day, but honestly, the best gift was waking up to your gentle nudges, urging us to start the adventure with swift and cheerful mood to see something new. Your fun-loving spirit turned even a rainy holiday into a joyful escapade. And in reflection, I'm so grateful for how you trusted us to lead while always having our backs or rather, our heels, as you followed us everywhere.

***

April 1, 2012, by early spring, we'd headed on the road towards south, and you, Sally, were our constant source of humor amid the bumps on our journey. In Alamo, Texas, at the Cesar Chavez Boulevard site, we dealt with a litany of campground complaints like leaky spigots, unclean facilities, and even gripes about "dogs too big" leaving poop behind. George and I chuckled because you, our medium-sized bundle of energy, were always so well-behaved. We'd look after you and oh, the stories we told! "Sally's just marking her territory for the next adventure," George would say with a wink, as you bounded around the shuffleboard courts, oblivious to the worn-out pool table and mismatched billiard balls in the clubhouse.

Your loyalty was evident when a severe storm dropped branches into the pool and you stayed right by my side as I navigated the soggy grounds, as your presence as a comforting anchor for me and George. Emotionally, you supported us through those minor frustrations; after a Thanksgiving meal that left me with a bout of diarrhea (blame the pork and ham!), you'd rest your head on my lap and your eyes full of unspoken empathy. George appreciated how you'd play and fetch with him to lighten the mood, your fun chases turning tense days into laughter ones.

***

From April 5 to 10, 2012, those were challenging days, Sally, when you were not good in health and your weight decreased as well. From April 5, as we parked at Cabela's in Buda, you diagnosed with diarrhea that lasted four long days. George and I were worried; you'd wake us at odd hours, dribbling and weak, and we'd clean up messes on sheets meant to protect the carpet. "Our girl is tough," George reassured me, but I could see the concern in his eyes as he helped to unyoke the tow dolly while you rested.

We provided dose to you with Imodium and heartworm prevention prescribed by Dr. Brumluwi, and slowly, your health perked up. By April 10, after a stay at Hwy 71 RV Park, you were eating regular food again like dry kibble in halves throughout the day. Your resilience taught us gratitude in those reflective moments; I'd stroke your fur and think how your loyalty mirrored our own commitment to each other. Fun returned when you'd chase the shadows in the park, and emotionally, you were our rock during Easter with the Fegans. As kids played and we chatted late into the night, you'd curl up at our feet, while offering silent support. Trust built stronger- we knew you'd bounce back, just as if we'd face any roadblock

58

together.

***

By midsummer on July 11, 2012, you'd had a small, normal "box," as George humorously called it, signaling your recovery. We limit you to dry food with half at breakfast, half later and even put on your muzzle to prevent scavenging decomposed critters that might have caused the upset. "Sally's our little explorer, but safety first," George said, laughing as you picked up sticks during walks, only to drop them at our command.

At the Pacific War Museum in Fredericksburg, you stayed cool in the RV while we toured, your well-being was always our priority. That evening, George roasted chicken with grated cheese for my birthday, and you got some taste of it and your tail wagging in gratitude. Your fun energy lifted us; emotionally, you provided comfort during long drives, your head on George's lap as he navigated the maps. Reflection brings tears of joy as your trust in us was absolute and a gentle reminder of the unbreakable bond we shared.

***

On September 12, 2012, Carlsbad Caverns Day was epic, Sally! We hiked the King's Palace and Big Room trails, but you waited patiently in the RV, staying cool with comfort. When we returned exhausted at 5:30 PM, your joyful greeting with barks and spins was pure fun to watch. "R. Sally's well," George noted in the journal.

You'd become our emotional anchor amid the scrubby landscape and rangy cattle, and your presence made the vastness feel intimate. We bought postcards, watched a movie on the caverns' origins, and reflected on white-nose syndrome in bats with your companionship sparked deep conversations about nature's fragility. Gratitude overflowed with your trust, turning a tiring day into one of loving and memorable day for me and George.

***

From April 14 to 25, 2012, our time at SKP RV "The Ranch" in Lakewood was a mix of dust and delight, with you at the center. Amid windstorms that coated everything in sand, you'd shake it off with comedic flair, sneezing dramatically as George laughed. "Sally's our desert warrior," he'd say. Your diarrhea returned again, but rice, bacon bits, and joint gravy powder nursed you back as loyal as ever, you'd still join happy hours and charming folks with your gentle demeanor.

Emotionally, you supported me through my own belly cramps and wounded feet; your head on my knee was a soothing balm. Fun came in walks around the large sites, where you'd chase scrub bushes, trusting us to guide you. Your presence fostered gratitude and teaching us to cherish simple joys irrespective of challenges ahead.

***

60

From May 18 to 20, 2012, journals shift to "Sully," but I know it was you, our Rosy Sally, perhaps an affectionate nickname George used. During the annular eclipse, you stood alert, paws down, ears lifted and sensing the cosmic shift. "Sully's our watchdog," George whispered. Your loyalty shone when coyotes appeared, and you stared them down with tail stiff and protecting us without any aggression.

Fun ensued as you followed trails, head high, exploring Mesa Verde's ridges. Emotionally, your steady presence during the descent winds offered support through your persistence mirroring. Gratitude for your trust as in those moments, we deepened our bond, a gentle reminder of life's fleeting wonders.

***

From September 10 to 30, 2012, in Albany's Hyatt's Green Acres, amid cornfields and gopher holes, your antics with a raccoon clawing the ceiling and George joking about "rent" for the bay. Your loyalty during quiet campfires, sharing war stories with neighbors, was heart touching moments.

In Iowa's Field of Dreams, you romped in the smaller-than-movie field and your fun chases lightening commercialized vibes. At Riverside RV Park, you'd watch barges on the Mississippi with your calm presence emotionally grounding us.

***

In October 2012, in Davenport, you'd stay cool during college visits and your wagging tail greeting us back. Fuel stops and rainy drives were bearable with your head on our laps for loyal support through winds and clouds.

In Missouri, at Ralls County Sheriff's Office, you'd pose for photos, adding humor to nostalgic reflections.

***

From December 9 to 13, 2012, our final days with you, Sally, were bittersweet. At Trout Creek RV Park, you'd weakened through cold extremities, affected breathing and bloated abdomen. We suspected a stroke or heart failure. George and I rushed Sally to vets, as her alert eyes trusting us till the end.

On December 13, you passed away, but your legacy endures for entire life. Loyalty in every step, fun in every chase and emotional support in every quiet moment. Gratitude fills me as being a true companion in the shape of pet. In reflection, Sally taught us true nature of love. George and I carry you forever as our faithful and ever-loving companion.

***

CHAPTER 8
STORMS AND STILLNESS
"She faced every storm with faith — and left me her peace in the stillness."

George, if our life together were a road map, this chapter would be the one with the squiggly lines and the detours through rain-slicked highways, the unexpected potholes of health scares, and those quiet stretches where the only sound is the hum of tires on dry pavement. We've weathered our share of storms, haven't we? Not just the literal ones, like that dust bowl whirlwind in New Mexico that turned our RV into a sandy shaker. But the stillness was the aches of aging bodies, the shadow of illness creeping in like fog over a morning lake, and the heartaches that test the glue that hold us together.

Yet here we are, still rolling along, your hand in mine and our faith in each other like a trusty compass. I look back with such gratitude, a gentle smile tugging at my lips, even with tears. Let's wander through these memories, shall we? With a bit of humor to lighten the loa because, darling, if we can't laugh at our creaky knees and misplaced glasses, what's the point of having adventure?

It started subtly, as these things often do. We were in our mid-sixties by then, the calendar pages flipping faster than the miles on the odometer. Remember that trip through Texas in

2012? The sun baked the earth like a forgotten loaf in the oven, and we were zipping along Highway 281, palm trees blurring like green sentinels. You'd just conquered that grueling hike up at Guadalupe Peak with height of 7,900 feet, and knees asserting louder than a squeaky wheel. "I'm fine," you grumbled, popping an aspirin with that persistent grin of yours. But I saw the wince, the way you favored your left leg as we unpacked at the RV park. Aging, I simply call it. I prefer to think of it as seasoning like a good wine, we were getting better, even if the bottle was more fragile.

That night, as we sat under the stars at The Ranch in Lakewood, New Mexico, a windstorm whipped up out of nowhere. Dust across the scrubland, rattling the RV like an angry ghost. "Hold on to your hat, love!" you shouted over the howl and pulling me closer. We laughed as sand sneaked through every crack, turning our dinner into a gritty surprise. But in the stillness after, with the wind dying to a whisper, we talked about the real storms looming in life. My right shoulder had been aching for weeks and sharp pangs that made lifting a coffee mug feel like hefting a stone. "Arthritis," the doctor in Austin had said, prescribing pills that rattled in my pocket like worry beads. You massaged it gently that night, your callused hands warm me for sure. "We've got this," you murmured. "Together, we're unbreakable." Your faith in me, in that quiet trust we built over decades, was my anchor. I leaned into you, grateful for the man who saw my pain not as a burden, but as another adventure to tackle side by side.

Of course, humor found its way in, as it always does with us. Remember Rosy Sally, our furry companion? That little Lebanese Doogie from Muskogee, how she aged right alongside us, her once-boundless energy slowing to a contented trot.

In Artesia, she had a bout of diarrhea that turned our RV into a comedy of errors. "Quick, the rice and bacon remedy!" I yelped, mixing up a lot while you chased her with a towel. She lapped it up, tail wagging weakly, and within days, she was back to her nosy self. But those moments reminded us of our own vulnerabilities. You'd tease me about my "previous mishaps" when I misplaced the RV keys in the fridge during a hot weather in Floresville. "Keeping them cool for the road?" you'd quip with eyes twinkling. I'd retort with your hiking mishaps, like vomiting at the peak from altitude sickness.

"My mountain man, conquered by thin air!" We'd dissolve into laughter, the kind that eases the sting of time's relentless march. Gratitude swelled in those moments; for you, George, who turned aging's indignities into shared jokes and strengthening our bond with every giggle and laughter.

But life's storms aren't always so light-hearted. There was that stretch in 2015, when we meandered through New York and Virginia, and illness hit like a sudden squall. My insomnia plagued me 36 hours awake, counting sheep until they formed a woolly army. "I'm grateful for you," I wrote in my journal that night, listing our blessings: family, health (mostly), and our cozy home on wheels. You held me through it; your steady breathing finally lured me to sleep.

Then came your turn. After a long drive to Bass Lake, you collapsed into bed, exhausted from extricating the dirtiness and sweeping debris. "Site unsuitable," you declared with mock authority, broom in hand like a knight's sword. But I saw the fatigue etching deeper lines on your face, the way aging whispered limits we once ignored. We faced it with trust and trust in God's plan and in our love's resilience. "We've traveled farther than this," I'd say, and you'd nod, faith shining in your eyes, George.

Sally's declining health mirrored our own brushes with fragility. Poor Rosy Sally had us rushing to vets, with Imodium and heartworm meds. "She's our practice run for old age," you'd joke gently, as we cleaned up messes at 2 AM. But when her heart failed in St. Augustine, it was no laughing that matter. I returned from touring the old fort to find her limp, extremely cold and struggle with breathing. We raced to the vet, your hand on mine as I drove, tears blurring the road. "Sally's been our faithful companion," you said softly, voice impenetrable with emotion. At the clinic, as she slipped away, we held her together, our grief with a shared storm.

In the stillness after, we clung to each other, reflecting on how illness strips away pretense, leaving only love's core. Gratitude for her life, for ours, washed over us like rain after drought. "We'll carry Sally's memory," you whispered, and I trusted that, just as I trusted you.

Aging brought more reflections, gentle waves lapping at our shores. In Carlsbad Caverns, we marveled at the ancient formations, but your knees prevented us from further steep paths. "Next time, we'll take the elevator," I teased, linking arms for support. You laughed, but there was truth in it. Our bodies, like the caverns' unstable bones needed care now. We faced life's storms with faith: in quiet prayers before bed, in scripture readings at campfire light.

Remember the annular eclipse in Mesa Verde? As the sun dimmed, coyotes howled, and Sully-wait, no, that was Rosy Sally's stand-in in my notes barked in confusion. We watched in awe, with your arms around me, trusting the light would return. "Like us," you said. "Storms pass, but stillness remained there." That trust, built over years of vows kept and roads shared, was our strength.

Through it all, humor was our lifeline. In Dubuque, Iowa, boondocking at Mystique Casino in freezing cold-"Too close to the crap stable," you quipped, shivering under blankets. Or in Moscow, Iowa, wrestling with gift card mishaps at breakfast. "Technology's aging worse than us!" I'd laugh, as the cashier fumbled. These moments, light and loving, wove gratitude into our days. I trusted your steady hand on the RV's staring during Texas thunderstorms, just as you trusted my intuition on alternative route. Reflection came in quiet times, like overlooking the Mississippi, where we'd sit, hands entwined, pondering life's ebb and flow.

As we aged, illness loomed larger. My shoulder pain flaring in San Antonio and your exhaustion after hikes in Guadalupe. But we met them with gentle resolve. In Albuquerque, amid panoramic views of Sandia Peak, we discussed our fears openly. "What if one of us..." I'd trail off, and you'd squeeze my hand. "Then we'll face it together, with faith." That trust, profound and unshakeable, turned storms into stories of triumph. Gratitude for each sunrise shared, for laughter echoing in the RV and for the stillness where love whispers brassiest.

Looking back, George, these years were full of storms and teaching us resilience and stillness, revealing our journey to explore the earth to view the stunning scenes together. We've aged gracefully, not despite the challenges, but because of trust in each other. Our faith in each other has been our guiding star. With humor to buoy us, gratitude to fill our hearts, and trust to bind us, we've navigated every challenge. And in the quiet moments now, I reflect everywhere together, forever. Thank you, my love, for being my support and keeping me calm in every challenge of life.

CHAPTER 9
HOME IS WHEREVER WE PARK
"Home was never the RV — it was her heart."

If there's one truth our years on the road taught us, it's that home isn't a fixed address on a map, George: it's the warmth we carried in our hearts, the laughter echoing in our little RV we affectionately called "Adventure." It was wherever we parked, under starry skies or beside bustling rivers, with our faithful companions Rosy Sally by our side. In this chapter, I want to revisit those moments, year by year, date by date, where we redefined home not as walls and roofs, but as the shared glances, the quiet gratitude, and the emotional anchors that kept us grounded through every twist and turn. You always said, with that gentle humor of yours, "Home is where the wheels stop rolling and where I get to hold your hand." And darling, how right you were. Let's wander back through those days and feeling gratitude at its highest level.

December 24, 2011, was our first Christmas in the RV felt like a cozy rebellion against the ordinary. We grilled that rack of pork under twinkling lights strung inside "Adventure," with Christmas carols playing softly from the TV. You surprised me with that Amish Heat Surge heater (destined for return, as you quipped, "Too hot for our already fiery love!"), and we lit tea candles and our makeshift luminarias glowing against the cold and wet night.

Rosy Sally curled up beside us, her tail thumping contentedly. That evening, as we sipped California wine and shared cherry chocolate, I felt a profound gratitude for the simplicity, for your steady presence. Home wasn't the house we'd left behind; it was this bubble of warmth we created, trusting that wherever we parked, we'd find joy in that place. Next day, laughing about our unconventional holiday. "Who needs a big tree when we've got the whole world as our backyard?" you said, pulling me closer. In that moment, I was grounded.

***

April 1, 2012, was the time when we cross into Texas, we navigated border inspections with ease. You are chatting amiably with the guards while I held Rosy Sally's leash tight. The heat climbed to 91 degrees as we rolled through palm-lined freeways, past herds of Brahmans grazing under relentless sun. We parked at Alamo's Cesar Chavez Blvd, complaining good-naturedly about the leaky spigot and the unheated hot tub at the campground. That night, as we reflected on the day's grievances (dirty pool tables, mismatched billiard balls), I whispered my thanks for your unwavering spirit. Home was our shared resilience, not the flawed facilities. We trusted the road to lead us right, and it did, grounding us in gratitude for the adventure unfolding.

On April 2, 2012, Dinner at Bill Miller BBQ in Floresville, with beef brisket that melted in our mouths, marked another simple joy. We boondocked in a parking lot, police patrolling but leaving us as we were. You tended to Rosy Sally's vet visit with such care, chatting with Dr. Brumluwi about her arthritis while I marveled at your gentleness. As we drove toward San Antonio, the overhead train of coal cars rumbling by, I felt emotionally anchored in your quiet strength. "Home is wherever we can park and breathe easily," you mused, and I nodded, heart full of trust.

April 3-5, 2012, when we headed toward San Antonio brought factory tours at SAS Shoes and visits to the O. Henry Museum, where we laughed over tales of embezzlement and escapes. Meeting the Fegans for lunch, then dinner at Kreuz Market BBQ (those pricey but "spendy" T-shirts!), we extended our stay at Cabela's lot despite noisy trucks. A hailstorm missed us by minutes, and as we huddled inside with garlic shrimp and Mexican pineapple, I reflected on our luck. Gratitude washed over me for these near misses, for your hand in mine during the chaos. Home transcended place was our emotional shelter that built on trust that we'd pass through any storm.

April 6-10, 2012, we landed on Propane runs and meat market hauls in New Braunfels filled our days, with Rosy Sally's diarrhea testing our patience (poor girl, muzzled to avoid mischief). Easter with the Fegans with ham, wine, and brownies felt like family, even in a non-gated home far from our own. We explored Lyndon B. Johnson Ranch, marveling at those white Lincolns, and Sauer-Beckman Farm, where history came alive. "Home is the stories we collect," you said softly, as we drove on. My shoulders ached, but your care grounded me, a gentle reminder of our shared vulnerabilities.

***

April 11-13, 2012, when the National Museum of the Pacific War in Fredericksburg captivated us for hours, from Nimitz's origins to WWII battles. You cooked chicken with grated cheese for my birthday, pistachio pudding pie sealing the sweetness. As we hiked Guadalupe Mountains (you conquer peaks while I waited with Rosy Sally), exhaustion hit, but gratitude for your adventurous soul kept me smiling. Parking at "The Ranch" in Lakewood, NM, amid dust storms and happy hours, we found home in the scrubby views and free popcorn movie nights. Trust in each other anchored us, even as my belly cramped and Rosy recovered.

***

On April 14-18, 2012, our tour of Carlsbad Caverns awed us with the Big Room trail, postcards, and origins film leaving

73

us breathless. "Curious about those bats," you pondered, tying into white-nose syndrome thoughts. Artesia brought antiques and boots, 91 degrees making me nauseous, but your humor lightened it. Home was our reflections, gentle and trusting, beyond any cave or desert.

***

May 14-18, 2012, from Abiquiú to Albuquerque, we traced canyons and rail runners, stopping at Santa Fe's Travel Center for vistas. Old casinos, art shows, and lakeside walks filled days with eclipse observations adding wonder. "Sully" (our nickname for Rosy that trip) sensed coyotes, her ears perking as we watched shadows play. Gratitude for nature's spectacles grounded us emotionally.

***

On May 20, 2012, we planned for Mesa Verde's Cliff Palace and annular eclipse day brought magic, coyotes crossing paths while we photographed ridges. "Home is this shared awe," I whispered, your arm around me.

***

On September 9-11, 2012, Freeborn County Fairgrounds to Clark Lorraine's birthplace, then Brampton, ND cluttered artifacts and quiet plains evoked reflection. Classic Cadillacs and toasty breakfasts added humor and trusting the road's destinies.

***

By September 29-October 2, 2012 – Mississippi River Valley views, Field of Dreams (smaller than the movie, but nostalgic), and Palmer Chiropractic College visits blended with history. Boondocking at casinos, cold nights, and hydraulic stops tested us, but appreciation for your problem-solving skills that grounded me.

***

December 9-13, 2012, when we landed on the streets of St. Augustine's forts, reenactments, and Fountain of Youth stirred history's echoes. But heartbreak struck as Rosy Sally's passing at Trout Creek RV Park. Lifting her cold body, pleading at vets, I felt unmoored. Yet, in reflection, home was the love we poured into her, the trust we'd built. "She's adventuring ahead," you said gently, anchoring my grief.

***

On August 3-31, 2015, we headed to Syracuse to Bass Lake, NY, with Marriott stays and Green Lakes camping. Doctor visits and campground requests wove through and your phone mix-up as "Reilly" sparking laughs with folks thinking you "Rall" from mysterious places. Gratitude for treated kindness, home in our aliases and shared secrets.

***

September 1-13, 2015, we left Bass Lake for Gettysburg, PA, via visitor centers and baseball museums. Big Buck Resort in Tennessee, then Little Rock, AR riverside parks and

75

Clinton's library. "Home is parked by history," you joked, trusting me as your loving wife.

***

On October 6, 2015, Casa Del Valle welcomed us as newcomers, Kelly and Donald's tour warming our hearts. Site 224 became our temporary haven, sweeping debris aside. Insomnia plagued me, but listing gratitude for family, health and our RV life grounded me. You, my emotional anchor, and made every park our eternal home with the feeling of peace in mind and heart.

George, weaving these dates together, I see how we defined home beyond any pin on a map. It was in the gratitude for sunrises shared, the humor in mishaps like leaky roofs or wobbly hikes, the trust that carried us through storms and sorrows. Our RV was our shelter, but you were my true grounding with the gentle voice reminding me we're everywhere together. Even now, our home endures in my heart, a reflective glow of eternal love.

Trust was key, you never wandered far, always by my side reminding us that home is wherever we were together.

CHAPTER 10
THE LAST HORIZON
*"The horizon we once chased now holds her light
— guiding me still."*

George, if I close my eyes, I can still feel the gentle hum of Adventure's engine beneath us, carrying us down those winding roads like an old friend who knows all our secrets. Our final journey together wasn't marked by grand destinations or checklists of sights to see. No, it was quieter, more intimate with soft unfolding of days where the miles blurred into moments, and the horizon seemed to whisper promises of peace. We didn't know it was the last one then, did we? But looking back, it feels like the universe wrapped it up just for us, with a bow of sunsets and laughter, tied neatly with the trust we'd built over all those years.

We set out our adventurous plan in October morning in 2012. Adventure loaded with the usual suspects: our favorite blankets, a stash of pistachio pudding pie (your guilty pleasure, remember?), and Rosy Sally curled up in her spot by the window, her tail thumping a lazy rhythm against the seat. You were behind the wheel, as always, your hands steady and sure, glancing over with that mischievous grin. "Ready for whatever comes, my love?" you'd say, and I'd nod, slipping my hand into yours. Trust was our extent-trust in the road, in each other, in the way life had always unfolded for us, one adventure at a time.

Our path took us south, meandering through the heartland, where the fields of Iowa and Missouri stretched out like golden quilts under the autumn sun. We stopped at those little roadside spots you loved the ones with homemade pies and quirky signs that made you chuckle. Remember that dinner in Dubuque, overlooking the Mississippi? You ordered the biggest stack of pancakes, drowning them in syrup, and teased me when I stole a bite. "Thief!" you'd exclaim, eyes twinkling, and I'd laugh, leaning in to kiss the sticky sweetness from your lips. Those moments were the glue and the gentle reminders of how we'd always found joy in the simple things. No matter the bumps, we trusted the journey to smooth them out.

As the days rolled on, we reflected on our legacy. Not in grand speeches, but in quiet conversations as the sun dipped low. You'd talk about the roads we'd conquered: the dusty trails of New Mexico, the lush valleys of Virginia, even that hilarious detour in Texas where Adventure got stuck in mud up to her axles. "We got her out together," you'd say with a wink, "just like everything else."

Our legacy wasn't in maps or milestones. It was in love we poured into every mile. We raised no empires, but we built a world of two plus Rosy Sally, of course, who taught us patience and unconditional wags. I think of how we'd pull over at dusk, set up camp under the stars, and you'd strum that old guitar, humming tunes from our early days. "Our song," you'd call it, even if the lyrics changed every time. Humor kept us light and trust kept us grounded.

But as we ventured further, the horizon began to shift in subtle ways. Your steps slowed a bit, your naps grew longer, but you brushed it off with that gentle humor of yours. "Just conserving energy for the next big hill," you'd joke, and I'd smile, trusting your strength as I always had.

We visited places that felt like echoes of our beginning: the serene banks of the Mississippi, where we'd once dreamed of forever, and the quiet parks in Arkansas, cotton fields whispering secrets to the wind. In those moments, we'd sit side by side, hands intertwined, reflecting on the laughter we'd shared. The time Rosy Sally chased a squirrel right into a pond, or when you tried to grill that "perfect" rack of pork and ended up with what we dubbed "charcoal surprise." Oh, how we'd giggle and turn mishaps into cherished stories.

Our final shared journey wove through the Deep South, where the air grew thick with humidity and history. We parked Adventure by the river one evening, the water lapping softly like a lullaby. You were quieter then, your eyes tracing the horizon as if memorizing it. "We've had a good run, haven't we?" you said, voice soft as the twilight. I nodded, leaning my head on your shoulder, feeling the steady beat of your heart against mine. We talked of love-not the flashy kind, but the gentle, enduring sort that weathers storms. "You're my anchor," I whispered, and you squeezed my hand, trusting me as you always had. Rosy Sally sensed it too, curling up between us with a sigh and her presence was a bridge of comfort.

As the days turned, challenges crept in like uninvited guests. Your energy waned, and we'd stop more often, turning what could have been frustration into opportunities for reflection. "Remember Alaska?" you'd say, eyes lighting up. "That kindergarten playground where we swung like kids?" I'd laugh, adding, "And you insisted on the biggest slide!" Humor was our shield and trust our sword.

We didn't dwell on the "what ifs"; instead, we savored the "what was." Our legacy emerged in those talks with the way we'd chosen love over fear and adventure over complacency. You'd pat Rosy Sally and say, "She's part of it too, our little family on wheels." And she was our loyal companion and testament to the trust we all shared.

The horizon drew closer in St. Augustine, that ancient city by the sea, where time feels eternal. We wandered the fort, hand in hand, marveling at the cannons and coquina walls that had stood for centuries. One night, as we sat by the fire, you turned to me, eyes full of that unwavering trust. "If this is the last horizon, know I've loved every mile with you." Tears came then, but they were soft, mingled with gratitude. We reflected on our journey: the roads that tested us, the love that sustained us and the humor that lightened the load. A tapestry of shared dreams, woven with threads of kindness, laughter, and unbreakable trust.

When the moment came, it was peaceful, like the sun slipping below the waves without fanfare. The way you'd make me coffee just right or pull over for a spontaneous dance under the stars. Humor lingered too: your terrible puns about "RV" up the fun, which I'd roll my eyes at but secretly adore.

Now, as we get older in age, the horizon feels different, but your legacy still guides me. Our journey taught me that love doesn't end; it evolves, carrying us forward. George, we're still everywhere together in the wind's whisper, the road's call, the gentle humor of memories. The last horizon wasn't an end; it was a peaceful goodbye. And so, I drive on, heart full, trusting the path as we always did. Forever, my love.

EPILOGUE

"Love never leaves; it only changes form — and she is still everywhere with me."

Now the road is quieter. The seat beside me is empty, but your presence lingers in every whisper of wind, every sunset over the horizon. I see you in the places we loved in the stillness of a lake, in the laughter of travelers passing by and in the glow of a campfire burning low.

I write this not in sadness, but in love. Because our journey isn't over, George. It just looks different now. Wherever I go, I will take or carry you with me.

Everywhere Together!

Forever!

ABOUT THE AUTHOR

George Reidy shared a beautiful life of love, laughter, and faith with his beloved wife. Together, they traveled across America in their RV, *Adventure*, discovering new places, meeting new friends, and finding the true meaning of home.

Everywhere Together: A Journey of Love and Adventure is her final love letter, a celebration of their shared life, their unbreakable bond, and the everlasting truth that love continues beyond the horizon.

www.ingramcontent.com/pod-product-compliance
Lightning Source LLC
Chambersburg PA
CBHW041630140626

46547CB00032B/2472